AGILE PROJECT MANAGEMENT

A STEP BY STEP GUIDE TO UNDERSTANDING THE AGILE PROJECT MANAGEMENT LIFECYCLE FOR BEGINNERS

Copyright © Richard Wall 2017
All Rights Reserved.

Table of Contents

Introduction 7

What Is Agile Project Management? 12

What Is The Difference Between Agile Project Management And Traditional Project Management? 20

Planning an Agile Project 30

The Events in Agile Project Management 46

The Scope of Agile Lifecycles 52

Understanding the Agile Lifecycle 54

The Need for Agile Project Management in Today's Market 80

Role of Leaders for Agile Project Management 92

Teamwork in Agile Project Management 95

Adopting Agile Project Management 104

Scrum Meetings and Procedures 109

Agile Project Checklist 116

Conclusion 120

Introduction

Good project management requires a special skill set from the project's team leader to actually apply all of the management principles which are detailed in this guide, to make sure that any project is completed on time, within cost and meets the given scope of the objective. It is critical for this individual to work with the team, motivating them to ensure the objective is achieved and within the deadline. A lot of obstacles may be strewn across the path to completion of the project which requires the lead to demonstrate strategic planning, quick thinking, and good communication to tackle these issues. These are the basic requirements of agile project management. A leader with these skills is required for the project, who can direct, control and monitors the activities of the team members. Team members get their direction and motivation from the leader to ensure that they complete all those tasks which have been assigned to them while collaborating with the leader and other team members.

This book helps you learn about agile project management with the complete involvement of every person and process necessary to build an understanding of how crucial it is to follow the trends of the market, to stay up to date and retain that competitive edge needed in business. You cannot expect a huge success suddenly unless you put in the hard work and agile project management requires consistent hard work with complete focus on the project. There are ways for you to get through any project with the guidance in this book, along with the entire implementation of the agile lifecycle. Each phase is explained in full detail which can help you to head in the right direction, even if you feel lost somewhere in between while developing those agile project management skills.

If your company is working with a traditional management system, then it is time to learn from this book and put these new processes into action. It will be beneficial for both the company and individuals, who can grow together to make a massive change in the marketplace. Technology changes every day, which is why staying on trend is necessary for each organization to survive in the modern market. You will be able to learn about the role of leaders in agile project management, along with knowing the relevant skills and techniques to be effective. It can be hard to adopt agile project management for those companies which have stuck to traditional management since the establishment of their organizations. Some people may resist, which is why there are some adoption techniques which will help you gain complete control over agile project management development and implementation.

The regular meetings which are a necessary part of agile project management are discussed thoroughly in this book, giving insight on what needs to be included in the agenda and what can be a waste of time if you speak of it within the short span of time allowed for a meeting. At the end of the book, there is a checklist which you can keep on file for your use while you are implementing agile project management for real. It is then ready to help you cross off some important steps, so you can be successful in completing any project.

There are still a lot of companies who believe that there is no need for agile project management and it will not bring any prosperity to them, but why would a company want to get to the lowest point and then rise with agile management? If you know the system of agile management beforehand, you would want to adopt it before you reach the point where it would be hard for everyone to adapt to it. The simple stages which are explained in this book will help you understand how it works and a consistent approach will take the company to new heights amongst the others which are already using agile project management.

Let's get started with understanding agile project management by looking at the detailed aspects of it.

What Is Agile Project Management?

Before you get started with a project, it is necessary that you have a proper understanding of what is involved so that you can deliver high quality work, full of content. Agile project management is a popular phenomenon developed by software project managers. It aims to deliver on projects at a lower cost and producing more effective results over a period of time. Due to the high pace of technological change in the market, software projects need updating rapidly to take advantage of any new developments, which makes the customers reach high in their demands. Customers are asked to plan ahead, indicating future needs before they wish to start the project so that there is a minimum delay in adapting to these. Agile project management helps in making such changes easier for the projects, even if there are some new requirements in the later stages.

Agile project management involves the activities and features of delivering added value work while keeping the three important factors of any project that is scope, time and cost. These three factors are managed in real time to ensure that value is created in the project. It reduces complex situations, by breaking the project lifecycle into separate portions, so that every portion can be completed before the deadline. It highlights critical segments and then tests the processes which need to be done for these to be achieved within a time frame of two to four-week cycles.

Agile project management has at its heart an aim to bring improvements in the project continuously as it proceeds, while being flexible, having complete team input and delivering high quality products or results. It has a scrum framework approach which is to build quality first and eliminate maximum wastage. Organizations can utilize the different tools and techniques available to the team to build agile management as this proves to be more effective. There are twelve basic principles which should be applied as a base for agile management delivering the information regarding the product, team, communication, and flexibility. These principles are known as the core values for agile project management which give the most effective implementation of any project.

The 12 Principles of Agile Management

Agile management principles support the concept of teams and their implementation in the project, which include streamlining the tasks and responsibilities to get the project completed easily.

1. One of the most critical principles underlying agile management effectiveness

is to ensure the customer's' satisfaction, by delivering consistent value and retention of clients. This is built around a continuous improvement process aimed at giving customer value to every segment of the cycle, without any interruptions or delays.

2. Another principle is that it can adapt quickly to any change in the environment, even if this comes late in the project, without causing harm to the overall results of the project or the competitors in the market.

3. Agile management works on the shortest possible timescale for delivery of results.

4. The people in the business and the project developers must work hand in hand to give the most effective results.

5. The project needs to be built around motivated individuals, while the project leads offer the support the team members need.
6. Have regular face to face conversations with all parties to tackle any issues and work as a team to help solve any problems as they arise.

7. Make sure to work within the software for progress and keep monitoring changes in the market.

8. A constant pace of work needs to be maintained by the developers, sponsors and the users for the sustainable development of the project.

9. All the team members need to pay complete attention to the project with a focus on good design and agility in enhancing technical excellence.

10. There is a need to maintain the simplicity of the objectives, without any deviations or complications.

11. A self-organizing team plays out the best in working together as good architects producing attractive designs.

12. The team behavior may need to be modified, with regular tuning in and reworking at intervals to achieve effective results.

There are advantages and disadvantages to agile project management which can change according to what comes along. It depends on the situation and the circumstances as to where you need to use this management style. The agile method works best when the customers and other stakeholders are involved with providing input, functional software support, flexible to change, accommodating to new ideas, and team players who collaborate well. If there is any change, the processes of the business can overwhelm and that is where you need agile project management in place to help support the adoption of changing parameters to the project. Here are some of the points which you can use to make it work for you.

Meetings on a Daily Basis

Daily meetings can be held, keeping the communication easy and open between the workers and the upper management for a smoother workflow.

Demonstration

Delivering live demonstrations to make the work understood by all while showing the progress in reaching the final product.

Sharing Feedback

Share the feedback with the team members, from both the stakeholders and the customers who are a part of this project and help the team work enthusiastically for the next iteration.

Stay Agile

Make changes to the project where needed to ensure it will be more effective and bring about any improvements by monitoring every step of the way.

What Is The Difference Between Agile Project Management And Traditional Project Management?

As mentioned earlier, there are two types of project management which remain on topic. Agile project management and traditional project management have slight differences which help in making a project more effective than before. As technology advances, these changes in the processes should be applied to make the outcome more functional.

Agile Project Management Vs Traditional Project Management

In the traditional project management, the manager is burdened with balancing the cost, scope, report, risk, and adaptation to change.

Whereas, when agile project management takes place, there are fewer main responsibilities which define the leads roles:

- The product owner has the responsibility to handle and set the project goals.

- He/she handles the schedule and scope of the project along with fulfilling the project requirements and setting priorities of the features required by the product.

- There is a scrum master who handles the team and makes sure the tasks are assigned with priority.

- The team members know their tasks and handle them on their own without any further support such as task assignment, progress reporting, quality control, detailed management and enhancement of product.

Traditional project management focuses on conducting a long plan with emphasis on every detail of the project, not knowing whether those details are necessary or not. The planning focuses primarily on the cost, scope, time and more, rather than the quality of the product and service to the client. A lot of time is spent in the planning which does not bring any return in the overall objective. As the environment keeps on changing, it requires quick actions and ideas to be implemented on the project, to fix any conflicts or to bring about improvements. Time is short and should not be wasted in the planning part of the project. There can be a change at any point which is why spending a lot of time on planning does not prove to be a successful step to completion. Whereas, agile management uses the approach for software development focusing on teamwork to get things done, bringing in any changes through the collaboration with customers. It responds to change quickly without any disturbance or harm to the overall project progress. Scrum is used commonly in agile management, which works on fast decision making and quicker processes and reduces the time spent on the unknown variables which are not so necessary for the project. These variables which have a chance to change in future, do not hold enough value, so giving them too much time is wastage.

Scrum emphasizes the delivery of a high amount of value to the customer in a shorter period of time, to achieve customer satisfaction and improve quality. Traditional methods focus on a linear process with long-term upfront planning and comprehensive documentation, which is of no use in the future environment. It organizes ahead of time, which is indeed good, but change is outmost in the projects where the planning may need to be modified at some point. Besides that, agile project management spends less time on planning and will only prioritize according to the features and requirements of the product, leaving the responsibility for this to the product owner. A small amount of work is divided among all which can be changed and updated when needed, according to the market demand, while the project is taking place. Customer collaboration is extremely important in agile project management during the developmental stage, to know whether any changes are necessary or not.

Here are some of the major differences between the two project management styles:

- Traditional project management is more rigid and directional, whereas agile is more flexible and adaptable to change.

- Easy communication is welcomed at agile, whereas traditional does much of this ahead of time, planning among the leads or product owners only.

- Management tells the workers what to do in the traditional management model and workers are given more autonomy to do their best work in the agile management style.

- Agile management is more fluid than traditional management.

- Agile management welcomes change, whereas traditional management resists change.

- Agile management gets involved with the customers, whereas traditional management does not connect with the customers until the project ends.

- Teamwork is enhanced in agile management but not in traditional management.

- Traditional focuses on serious processes whereas agile methods are less formal and so can be flexed rapidly as things proceed.

- Traditional management favors the "anticipation mode" whereas agile management favors the "adaptation mode".

- Daily meetings are held in agile management for open communication amongst all parties and meetings are less frequent and more splintered in the traditional management model.

- Agile management breaks things into sections with short spans and small practices whereas traditional beliefs in long processes with details.

- Agile management is unplanned and analyses processes on a continuous basis.

- Agile management has a mindset or philosophy that looks for focused thinking, vision, an incremental framework, customer value and easy to understand processes.

- Agile management is more of a pragmatic and test driven approach rather than traditional management.

- Agile management receives feedback throughout the cycle with the intention of ensuring the final result fits the client's' needs and expectations, where the traditional model presents a finished solution.

Agile project management shares many similarities with the traditional management process but looks to improve on it through breaking the work into quicker and shorter processes, along with involving everyone in them throughout the life of the project. It makes each process and the value to be gained from it clear to the people who are involved while trusting them with their contribution to the work.

Traditional project management works on a long-range analysis of value added, without keeping everyone in the loop which does not produce high quality results anymore. It is slow in processes and due to not adopting changes along the way, it can fall behind the competitors in the market. An agile management system can validate the business bringing more value than the traditional management, which along with receiving a continuous feedback helps in improving the processes to reach to an effective result, staying focused on the customer's vision and business value.

Planning an Agile Project

An agile project may seem easier to plan but it is the team which works as a backbone for any project. If the team is dedicated and the timing well planned then there is nothing which can interrupt the project and prevent its successful outcome. As agile project plans build in some flexibility for changes to enhance the quality, there will be new elements added to the project through different ideas generated by a diverse team. Besides the overall organizational planning, the people planning plays a vital role in this aspect of an agile project, which can only benefit the company and the outcome. Planning an agile project involves certain stages, people, and the owners, but with the aim of diving much more quickly into the implementation phase of the project and not crossing every T and dotting every I of the lifecycle beforehand. Understanding of the planning stages is important to implement the project in an efficient manner. Here are some of these stages discussed as follows:

Stage 1: Product Vision

The product owner needs to have good product vision, in that he knows exactly where and how he sees the end product functioning and fitting his requirements. He/she needs to have full awareness of the product and how it will be supportive to the company's strategy. The focus should be on who will be using the product and this vision needs to be revisited at least once in every three months for the consistency and retention of the customer's goals.

Stage 2: Product Roadmap

The owner of the product is meant to create the product roadmap, defining the high-level view of it which will fulfill the requirements. He/she will mention each requirement within a loose framework and the estimated time to get them completed. First, the identification will be done and then it will be prioritized accordingly. A rough estimation will be made to complete the roadmap and how long it will take even if there have to be some changes in between. For larger or longer-term projects, the roadmap should be revised two or three times in the project's lifecycle.

Stage 3: Release Plan

The third stage identifies the release plan which defines how and when the software which they are working on is moved into the live environment. There will be many releases within the agile management cycle so the segment that is released first must be prioritized. There are about three to five sprints in a cycle typically, but the plan must be established first.

Stage 4: Sprint Planning

The master of the product makes the sprint plans which are also called iterations. The product starts by determining each of these iterations and the planning of the sprint takes place before it starts. The scrum team makes sure to cover all the necessary measures to achieve the desired result before it starts with the iterations.

Stage 5: Daily Meetings

Daily meetings help the team to learn about new things and information which one may otherwise miss out on or forget. It updates the team with what has been done and what is still outstanding on a daily basis. It should be no more than 15 minutes every day, before the scheduled work for that day starts. Roadblocks, conflicts, problems are highlighted during this meeting every day by the product owner and the team.

Stage 6: Sprint Review

At the sprint review stage, the demonstration of each product segment is made to the stakeholders, identifying if any changes are necessary or it should be finalized and ready for launch. The entire process is explained briefly to the product owner for his complete satisfaction.

Stage 7: Sprint Retrospective

This is the stage where the team pulls in for the meeting to discuss how the sprint process went and what problems they may have faced. They discuss the problems and how to improve them for future. It gives a complete comprehensive review of any improvements to the product to the stakeholders. This meeting is held after every sprint is achieved.

Who is Involved in Agile Project Management?

Agile management takes a mix of corporate people to complete a project effectively and efficiently. The team is made up of qualified and professional people who have five main roles as described below:

Product Owner

The product owner is also the lead for the project and product and the bridge between the customers, stakeholders and the team. He/she is responsible for initializing a new product to the market to improve business processes or take advantage of new technological developments.

The product owner is an expert at taking care of the customer's needs and values their views. He makes sure that their requirements are addressed and prioritized to provide them with quality products. The product owner makes sure the team is on track, keeping open lines of communication on a daily basis and shields the members from any organizational noise or disturbance. He/she is also known as the "customer representative" who the customers trust and depend upon when making a purchase. The product owner has the power to make strategic decisions on a daily basis through the life of the project.

The Team Members

Agile project management works with the team members, who collaborate with each other and know how to coordinate the processes to get the work done efficiently. Each of them is an expert in their field, knowing what they have to do and how to get it done on time. In software development, there are developers, testers, writers, engineers, programmers and other important roles. All these roles must coordinate and work with each other to provide coherence and support to follow the goal of the project and reach it on time. The team is made up of diversified workers having various skills allowing each of them to handle a variety of different aspects at the same time, but working to a common project goal.

Scrum Master

The Scrum Master is the main support for all team members, who makes sure that all the roadblocks are clear and there is no vagueness in understanding what needs to be done. He keeps monitoring progress and works as the project facilitator as well. He works side by side with the product owner, reporting progress and provides an effective leadership to the team.

Stakeholders

Anyone who has an interest in the project is a stakeholder, whether from within the organization or outside. Even the end customers are stakeholders as they will depend on the product and use it. They are not responsible for the product but are affected by the outcome of the project. This group can include people from different areas of expertise or other companies. In agile project management, the support for customers and the project team is essential for the continuous improvement philosophy which brings greater results.

Agile Mentor

An agile mentor is someone who has experience of using the agile project management methodology before, where he/she does not need the training to understand the process. The mentor knows all the strategies and rules for allowing feedback to come in freely. The mentors are not responsible for looking after the progress of the project, but only making sure that the plan is progressing. He/she cannot direct and has no formal authority over team members but can convey the approaches and techniques of agile project management.

How to Track the Project?

Tracking the project is necessary for transparency and the measurement of value added to the product. If there is no monitoring, then it can result in negative circumstances for the company that is executing the project. Here are some of the ways to track progress in agile project management:

Vision Statement

A vision statement needs to be created regarding the product and how it will benefit the company. It is a quick summary of the product along with matching it to organizational strategies and how it can improve profitability. It should include an outline of the main goal for the company and how agile management procedures will be implemented to achieve this.

Roadmap

Again, a roadmap of the product and project needs to be reviewed once a week to see if everything is on track and on time. It needs to connect with the vision and goal of the company giving the time frame for each stage as well.

Backlog

The backlog is the list of the products, features, and requirements which have been defined on a prior basis and where these are still outstanding. It needs to be updated every day following a review of what work has been done on the day and what is still left to be completed, indicating whether the project is on track to be completed by the deadline or not.

Release plan

A complete timetable of scheduled releases of software at the different stages of the project as it is developed. This should be reviewed on a weekly basis to the team on track and identify major milestones achieved in the project lifecycle.

Increments

Keeping track of user responses when each stage or increment of the project is completed and how the customers have preferred it and if not then why. Receiving feedback after each increment is necessary to generate improvements in the next sprint release.

Using each of these processes in the tracking of a project will ensure value is constantly being added to the product and it is staying on target. It is something that should be done on a daily basis. These ways will help in ensuring the focus on the project's goals will be kept and prevents team members getting lost in between releases. Where all the team can track progress so knowing exactly what still must be done and what has already been achieved throughout the entire project will generate confidence in the leader. This also allows everyone to know their job and that they are doing it the right way which will surely make the result more successful.

Agile management is not about tracking the project to make sure that everyone is doing the work right, but to make sure that the team is on track to reach the deadline and finish the product on time. Most of the time, teams are well trained, especially for the bigger projects, which is why it is less about looking for the skills gaps. Where teams are initializing on the project having an agile system for the first time then you do need to keep track of this knowing that not everyone would be willing to accept it all of a sudden. Some of the people may resist change in the management and working style. It is a completely different dynamic from the traditional management which is why it would need mentors to help the people accept it and go along with it over the traditional system, to make the project successful.

The Events in Agile Project Management

There are certain events which occur in agile project management which you have to focus on while you are conducting a project. It helps in the product development if you follow these accordingly and the given results are better, there will be profitable and positive results by the end. Here are few of the events which you need to focus on keenly:

Project Planning

Every project requires planning and so do those using an agile project management method. It does not require a detailed and lengthy plan but a quick briefing needs to be done in a written form to have a record of defining the goal, vision and the expected end results. A roadmap needs to be discussed among all the team so everyone is on the same track and knows what they are doing and why they are doing it. A clear understanding of the plan should be given to everyone before the project starts.

Release Plan

A target date or deadline needs to be given to end the project and provide positive results. This includes identifying the product features and requirements necessary to meet this deadline. The launch date needs to be announced from the beginning so everyone keeps the pace to the appropriate level for getting all the work done on time.

Sprint

The functionality of the product needs to be discussed among the team members working with each other to make sure that they are on the same understanding and the development phases. The iterations should not be more than four weeks each and should be launched on time. There should be the same length for each sprint, making sure to complete the project entirely on time. The team needs to plan amongst themselves how to manage this and what needs to be achieved for each one.

Sprint Planning

Meetings should be conducted before the team starts working on the next sprint. As the management holds a meeting with the customer, a separate meeting of the team members needs to be conducted as well with the agile mentor and scrum leader. They need to define the roles and goals to each other, so they know everyone is working on relevant tasks sharing the same goal in their minds. Each task needs to be reported to the scrum leader by the end of the day so that he/she can make sure that certain tasks are completed and do his/her job correctly as well.

Daily Scrum

There should a daily meetup of all the team members with the product owner each morning to review what has been completed and who needs to do more. A quick outline should be given of what needs to be completed by the end of the day and how much time is left to completion. The meeting should not be more than 20 minutes every day but needs to be conducted on a daily basis.

Understanding agile project management is not hard but when it comes to implementation, even a professional can find it difficult because of the diversity of people and personalities at a single workplace. Each task should have a professional or expert to finish it completely to ensure the quality of the product. If there are any new staff hired, they should be well trained and made aware of the goals. Any problems need to be identified by the scrum leader and the mentor to manage them during the project and they can provide motivation to get things done to provide full satisfaction to the customers.

Customers are the key to every business nowadays and once you understand their needs and fulfill them well, then that product can flourish in the market. If you do not pay attention to the customers then the project can be a huge loss for the company, wasting all the effort which the people put into it. Keeping in mind the three factors of cost, scope and time; a project can be a broken into a series of tasks which need to be handled and managed with techniques that are applicable according to the demands of the market and technology.

The Scope of Agile Lifecycles

The scope of agile lifecycle can vary from company to company or project to project. When the entire business works towards the development, this can later be turned into effective feedback for the company. The development of solutions is complicated, yet it has to be broken into procedural steps which show the construction cycle. The main result is at the end when there is success in the project and it no longer needs to be modified or changed.

There are many lifecycles which are described under the agile management with the scrum construction being one of these. Here, the agent of agile project management makes sure to prioritize the stacks/backlogs, bringing them into the current iterations. The stakeholders are involved through the process of acknowledging their feedback to verify the work and ensure things are going well as it moves along. Daily scrum meetings are held in this lifecycle for the team to be updated regarding any new information or where the tasks have been completed by the team members.

While this lifecycle does prove to be an effective one which is why a realistic lifecycle has been generated to cover it under six phases; conception, inception, construction, transition, production, and retirement. These six phases explain the entire agile management project to anyone. It works in a similar way for every sprint as each is about to come into the process.

Understanding the Agile Lifecycle

Concept Phase

This is one of the tough phases where you have to do the pre-planning regarding the sprint which you are about to launch. There is a target at the beginning of every project which you must achieve and that is done by building the overall concept of the solution. Here there are the critically important things which you need to determine in this phase to provide guidance for work further in the project:

Define the Business

When defining a business, it is necessary to have the market concern and the bigger picture of the business strategy in your head. You have to consider what new functions will improve your business in the market to enhance the presence of your organization. There is a need to determine the potential profitability of the project and how it can help the people who are working in the organization. Also, to look at the impact of the project in the market and in the organization, especially on those who you are going to direct to complete the project. This is essentially the exploration part which needs to be short and brief without any elaborations. You do not have to invest so much time on the project within the conceptualization but just write down the points will help you get to the business potential. You can follow a good strategy with the identification of the scope and goals with the potential stakeholders as well.

Strategy for the Project

A well-built strategy always helps you to reach the endpoint, with minimal changes needed to improve it or to make it look better. There may be many issues which come out as you draw out the strategy in more detail and you will have to answer several questions on your own, such as who will be leading the team? How will the subject of project matter to the organization? What will be the iterations? The geography? Location? Development? And more will come along. The team needs to be allocated and consider different staff combinations which seem possible or feasible for you as the leader for agile project management. As there are a lot of possibilities, you then need to select out of the abundance of options to make a final decision for the team which will be handling future iterations.

Feasibility

You need to prepare a feasibility report for the conceptual phase where you see the suitability of the project and whether it can be established in the market in future or not. This aims to identify whether your investment will be fruitful or not so that you do not end up wasting the costs and time of your business and the team. Every project requires effort which is why it is necessary that you recognize and make sure that such efforts are being focused on the right task. A lot of people make the mistake of not doing thorough research on the feasibility report and think that if they must invest more, they will do it in the inception phase which leaves no structure and you this can increase the financial cost of your project.

You have to keep four main things in mind when you are preparing the feasibility report which is that you need to assess the project in terms of the technical feasibility, economic, political and operational feasibility. This full feasibility analysis needs to portray the risks and the opportunities which will come along as you go further in the project. The criteria will be defined with the help of a feasibility report when you develop the full scope of the product. It also helps you to recognize whether it is worthwhile to start the project or you should stop the planning right away, where there is any negative impact on the organization at its initiation. Therefore, it is essential to question the feasibility throughout the project when you review regularly through the lifecycle.

The concept and feasibility activities need to be undertaken as quickly as possible to ensure that you are able to convince the stakeholders of the project's desirability and usefulness and make sure that everyone is on the same track to the end goal. When there is enough funding and motivation in place, you can then take the potential project further, working with team members and collaborating on the next stages.

Inception

This phase is directly linked with the project initiation, where you can refer to it as the first week of starting the project. It can also be referred as iteration 0 or the warm-up for the project where you give an initial push to get things moving along. There are certain ways where you can initiate the project such as:

Funding

When you have prepared the portfolio for the project and have engaged with management to bring it to inception, this is the time where you negotiate the funding for the project to start. You must think how you are going to get the funding and from where, with a realistic point of view. The cost, duration, location and all the other key factors need to be analyzed when you are ready to pitch for funding. All these factors need to be reasonable and practical with a good justification for any assumptions on viability, so you can get the permission and the funding to start the project, as shown in the feasibility report.

Stakeholders and the Scope of Project

Under agile project management, it is necessary that you bring the stakeholders alongside you when you are starting the project. You need to work with them to make them understand the logistics of the system and the initial requirements of different models, identifying what they are looking for. At the stage of iteration 0, you need to have a high level of communication with the stakeholders, using tools such as whiteboards and index cards to model the project and to reach successful solutions which are beneficial for both the stakeholders and the company. The model brainstorming needs to be done with the stakeholders for them to understand the cycles, so they can better support you in achieving the goals. It gives confidence to the stakeholders as well as the company that they are heading in the right direction.

Team Building

Next and the most important step of initializing the project is that you build the team which can work together in the organization to reach the planned goal, rather than their own personal goals. You can identify the members who will be a part of the project, having some of the senior developers as well to coach the project team, keeping staff on track. There needs to be a diversity of workers in the team according to the mix of tasks an iteration demands. Each role needs to be assigned to the person who is expert in the necessary field.

Initial Architecture System

You need to have a good picture of how you are going to operate the system. Once you have this understanding then the project will be able to move in a clear direction otherwise it will be a waste of time and effort. The mainframe of the project needs to be clear with the developers on the potential project working with the architecture of the system. The architecture needs to be referred to again and again so that each detail of development can be reached within the shortest time span. You can also develop some documentation from it which you can keep as a record, but that is not the point, you look to work on the design of development cycles in each session for effective results.

Setting the environment

There needs to be the provision of all necessary tools and equipment to get the work done well and efficiently. A proper environment can motivate the team allowing them to work with enthusiasm and autonomy. The development tools, working area and the collaboration of team is important. It is not necessary that all the tools are available from the start but get the basic ones together to kick start it and then you need to add in more hardware and equipment as needed for each sprint or iteration to move further.

Estimating project

When you have gathered all the information and started the project, estimate the project lifecycle and target again to make sure that you are staying streamlined and not off the track. After the architecture, design and environment building, you then review the estimation of the agile project which can then evolve over the entire period to project completion.

Construction – Development of Iteration

The main part of the project is where you construct the iterations, developing high quality software that meets the needs of the stakeholders and everyone else who is involved in the project. The agents of agile project management need to understand that each step is crucial at this phase. In order to complete the construction phase successfully there are certain points which you need to know as per the following:

Collaboration

Here you have to achieve a good collaboration between the team members and the stakeholders to avoid any big risks or errors in the project. When you have good affiliation with the stakeholders and developers, it helps you in communicating with them easily, get their reviews and feedback to improve throughout the cycle. You have more chances of improvement between iterations when you have close collaboration.

Implementing Functions

There is a chance of change in the requirements of the customers if they wish to make improvements in the product during the cycle. There could be some new discovery that they would like to add into their project. With the flexibility of agile project management, we can make changes in the processes during the later development stages as well. Preparing the team members for this challenge is important at the initial stages of the cycle so that it does not take time for them to accept that they have to work with the demands of the stakeholders, rather than a given plan which they can stick to across all work to complete the project. Accepting change is required for continuous improvement and that is what makes agile project management better than the traditional style of project management, which is not so effective nowadays in meeting the demands of the market. You have to give up some control for the scope of the project to the stakeholders, along with the budget and schedule at the same time. They can take their time in making changes before it ends, they can make the changes however they wish to.

Designing and Analyzing

As an agile agent, you are required to analyze the needs of the stakeholders and what kind of model they are looking for before you start implementing the design. You must think over all their requirements and see if there is anything else needed, according to your own expertise by sketching out the design to your own satisfaction. Often, sketched diagrams are used to display the design and then changes can be made on to this chart easily, adding the requirements for the later stages as they change in between. The test-driven designs are also initiated in this phase of designing to see the development of each iterative for testing and producing the code for fulfillment of the test. The complex requirements of any issues with the designs can be thought out and there can be further changes if required in future.

Ensure the Quality

As the project goes along, it is important to keep on monitoring whether the project is in line with the customer's requirements or not. There are guiding codes which can help the agents to learn about the quality of the project and if you have done a similar project before then you will know the quality concerns and issues. You have to ensure that the best design is being created by the team members and ensure that there is no lacking in the quality and functionality.

Working Solutions

You have to keep on providing solutions for the problems which may arise throughout the project. Ensure that the regular delivery of work is being achieved through the development cycle and the collaboration within the team is optimized and that they are focused on the product. There may be solutions which can be sorted out by the team. These solutions need to be tested before they get implemented by the team members. Testing the solutions makes it easier when you are demonstrating the product to the stakeholders to ensure they are satisfied.

Testing Again

A great amount of testing needs to be implemented while you are working with the agile project management cycle to ensure the best quality and design of the product on completion. When you test the product at each iteration, it enhances your own learning as well to confirm in the testing process your confidence in a certain solution for the product before it goes into the market, so the next time a sprint comes in you are ready to go immediately into it. The specifications which are given to you need to be confirmed within the software that you have made in each iteration at the ideal rate of testing and the developers need to follow the full requirements for testing it with the professional users. You cannot establish the product in the market without testing it because then you risk the trust of the stakeholders. This would be a failure after investing the cost and time over the project.

Here are a few steps which will guide you on the testing of iterations:

First, you have to define the test criteria and then run through the program testing each new development of the iteration against that criteria. Keep running through the tests until it shows a "pass" sign which means you do not have to go further. You will be able to see the changes in the software and the program. If it fails, then you need to add in a few steps further for you to make whatever changes are needed in the system and the program and then run the tests again. When it passes the process of testing then the development for this iteration ends and it is ready to be delivered to the stakeholders.

Transition

This is basically known as the "End Game" which is deployment. Here, you release the solution and test it live, improving the product where required. Most of the time there will be something which you would want to change or improve after live testing which is why it is recommended to go through a transition phase of agile management. Even if the live test does not fail, it is required that you re-check through the transition phase. You must look into several aspects when you are going through the transition phase, as follows:

Final Testing

The system needs to be tested at the end for full acceptance where there are no more modifications required, and it is ready to be given to the stakeholders who have invested in your services to provide them with it. You need to run a regression test to see whether it works or not. You can also run a pilot test to see the eventual results for users which will help you learn from feedback on the product.

Rework– If Needed

If you think you need to rework over parts of the system at the last stage, then you need to do the testing and do not ignore this since it will impact on your reputation and the service you provide to the stakeholders from the company. If any defect is found, it can ruin the image and the stakeholders may not come back to your company for similar services on their products or projects. You have to fix all the defects which are visible to you and then finalize the system.

Finalization

The last step of the process requires you to submit the documentation covering the entire procedure of iterations which can include the notification that there is no need for any further rework. It works as an authentication with the full details that you have gone through for the entire procedure with logical reasoning to achieve the project according to the needs of the stakeholders as told. There should be priority requirements, cost, investments and all other details need to be mentioned with a full report. How the project will be earning the money and how it can bring benefit to the market should be mentioned at the same time with a complete analysis.

Training

Next, is the step where you will need to train the users on these improvements or where there is a lack of information or knowledge regarding the sprints or the system. A leader can analyze this while working with the team so they can identify the strengths and weaknesses and work on their lack of knowledge for implementation of the service. The entire staff needs to be trained through various means of hands-on experience, workshops and mentoring to get the best from the project result.

Deployment

The deployment part is where you do not share the information regarding the system with any third party. The system remains within the organization but cannot be used for any other company other than the one which you have worked with. You have to keep it in a safe place it is accessible for only few leader positions after getting done and delivering the product to the stakeholders. It remains within the stock of the system, but no one has the access to it other than the leads.

Production Phase

The production phase is similar to the feedback phase where the system is deployed and handed over to the customer, however, at this time some of the team will work with the stakeholders if needed.

The goal is to keep the product updated and to see whether the users are finding it interesting and that it works according to their needs. The support needs to be available to the stakeholders at this time because different team members each have their expertise and know where they have contributed and how they can sort things out if the users get stuck somewhere in the system. If there is an upgrade in the system which has been used previously by the stakeholders then it is necessary that an automatic update is also sent to the stakeholders, for the smooth running of the system and compliance. Even if there are multiple iterations on which you are working on, the ongoing feedback and support need to be available all the time for the release of the systems.

Retirement

Retirement is when the entire product is deleted from the system of the company and removed from memory as well. This happens when it has held as data for years and no one has referred to it requesting an upgrade or support. It becomes obsolete and should be removed automatically when it is inactive for a few years, making more space for the upcoming iterations and developments of the company. It has a strong impact on the organization when a new system takes the place of an outdated one, which can complicate the procedures as well. The retirement phase should not have a huge impact on the operations of the businesses except in regard to any legacy issues. It can be removed on the condition that there is no support needed regarding it, it is more than five years old, it has become redundant or obsolete, has no recent feedback, or it has been replaced with a new system or iteration. These are some of the conditions where it can be removed from the system, otherwise, it needs to stay in the system for future reference or evidence if any problem arises. Most of the time, older releases are given back to the same company to update a system which can be the reason for removing the old one and replacing it with a new one which can be an assurance that you have completed the project for the company.

The Need for Agile Project Management in Today's Market

One of the most common misconceptions among the traditional project management users is that they do not need to follow agile project management methods since it can make little or no difference for them but how is that possible when the name is different, the procedures would be different if you train the team members and work together with customers throughout a project's development. An easy way to understand agile project management is that it is much more self-organized and the rapid pace which is achieved through shorter iterations prove much more effective for longer-term projects as well. There are certain managers who have suggested that the agile project process does not need management but if not then some supervision, guidance, and motivation are required for good agile project development.

Critical project success has agile project management behind it and the processes matter when the team members are working together with the right mixture of skills and personalities. If the team's skills combine well, then there is nothing better than that to help deliver a value-added and quality product to the stakeholders. Agile management helps to formalize the processes of dividing it into segments, encouraging people to collaborate and interact more than having them sitting in isolation while doing the work. Collaborating helps them in sharing ideas, encouraging improvement in design features as well. All the team members have the same vision for their work which is delivered to them by the product owner, who has complete information and knowledge of the product. That person is directly linked with all the other stakeholders involved in the project. If the project needs to be delivered at a high level of quality, then everyone needs to understand the same vision and encourage the teams to work together.

Most drivers for the processes are advocated where the vision is communicated within the meetings and other inputs provided by the customers. Maybe there is the need for some planning but if the team all have lists of tasks and procedures assigned to them, they will know what they have to do without having any major obstacles created, which directly link to the main goal of the company. The plan needs to be affiliated with the project goals so that everyone can connect with it while working on their tasks. When the vision is shared with all the team every day, it works as a guide for them to get done with the work efficiently, knowing that they must stay on track and if that is not the case then get off the track somewhere in between. This is why it is important that the vision is mentioned in the daily meetings, which are held by the leads for 15 minutes every day.

The vision formation is not the sole responsibility of the project manager or the owner of the project, but all the team members can take some initiative to build a vision which they can improve on for the benefit of the company. The vision may also come from other stakeholders such as the customers which you can implement and allow more chances of improvement while working with each other. Rather than having a detailed comprehensive written purpose, you can simply have it written in a form that everyone can relate to. Even if the team wants to add their own visions which can drive them to work effectively, they should have the autonomy to do so under an agile project management system. Great results can be generated when you have collaborations and when there are frequent discussions regarding the project and are more likely if you stay away from a command and control plan which does not work anymore. The layout of the project needs to be defined for everyone so that there is a mutual understanding of the emergence and the adaption of the entire project, which is going to be run by all the members and gains mutual consent, so all the team members can work on the same vision. The main nurturing of the project begins when everyone in the company understands how important the project is and how it can benefit all of them, achieved through dedication and hard work.

It is obvious that no project comes along without some obstacles which is why you need to be prepared for any challenges which you may face while completing the project. There will be some obstacles which can be irrelevant and you can ignore these so they do not waste time, whereas there will be some crucial ones which you have to sort out so that they do not disrupt the plan more in the future. It is dependent upon the leader and his experience to know how it can affect the goal while working on the project and what needs to be done to make the path easier. Participating in agile project management is a huge success in itself because it is really hard to retain and manage all aspects with the calmness that is required by the lead.

A good team can quickly manage to decide on the features and divide them amongst those with the right expertise for each of the iterations, again whilst keeping to the deadlines. There have to be tasks done by the end of each day to make sure that everyone is on track, doing something which they have to report to the agile agent to show progress. This will keep everyone focused, knowing that the project will be done on time, making any corrections if needed at the testing phase before delivering it to the stakeholders.

Another type of obstacle which you may face is that some team members will take their time to adjust or adapt to the flow with the rest of the team. A person may be having a hard time in adjusting into the team or may resist change. Most of the time, the developers will not be a problem, but if there is someone who could be creating an obstacle in the project then training is necessary, along with guidance. As a leader, it is your responsibility to support the team member and help him in learning about agile projects as this can create a disaster for the project itself.

Counseling sessions may need to be held with a team member, along with the on the job coaching which can guide the individual step by step in expressing concerns to other team members and encourages them to help each other to complete the project as a team. While choosing the team members, it is essential that you are aware of all the people who are in the roles and able to give their full contribution to the project. Everyone in the team should be working together and the performance for each can be measured by the agile mentor who is there to observe and help the individuals with any difficulty they may face during the project. It is best that the problems of any team member not adapting remains between the manager and the team member.

In some companies there can be at least one dysfunctional area which can hurt the programming or the standard of the software. There are projects which work instantly with full commitment from everyone, but those projects are not all likely over the longer term. A leader's responsibility is to ensure that all projects can work in the long run, as he is the motivator for the team. It is not just about getting the work done within a few weeks by taking on smaller projects.

Agile project management does not mean that you take the projects which have shorter deadlines but is more about how effective the results are based on this management style, fulfilling the deadlines and providing quality work from the team as well.

The productivity of the team depends upon the possible solution which the manager provides along with making sure that the work is completed by the delivery dates for the software submission. A project manager should know all the ins and outs of the product along with discovering what is needed, researching for information if they are doubtful of something or are lacking the knowledge.

Agile project management is not free of politics, as politics exists in every organization. There are some under agile project management as well, competing with the new ideas and especially when the team members are not able to understand each other, or they do not get along well initially. The ideas for projects could be different, diversity, resources, too many deadlines, work pressure and a lot of other factors can create a space for politics to rise easily. When the manager has agile mechanisms in place then the politics can be minimized but they cannot be eliminated completely. Regular communication where the goals are made clear to all provides less chance of having some kind of politics and if it still exists then this may be due to the personality mix.

Agile project management is both leading and serving at the same time, which helps you get the idea in the clearest way. Agile management works as a contributor for the teams to function efficiently in getting on with the project and the leader learning along with them. A project plan does not need to have all the details described and these have to be followed rigidly, because it may not be the best fit for all the people who are working on the project. The team members do need the autonomy to do good work and use their skills to perform better.

The organizational structure is more horizontal than vertical with the only difference and preference given to the project manager is that they direct and help the team out by supervising, knowing the process best among all the members due to their experience and authority. There is a sequence of activities which are assigned and the vision is set out to all the team members to understand it in the best way possible. The project manager needs to remove any obstacle which may come along for the completion of the project so that the team members can work with complete ease. The project manager works at ensuring that he protects the team from any outside disruptions and all the obstacles are removed so they are not able to have any impact on the team members.

Role of Leaders for Agile Project Management

The fundamental idea of self-driven teams is a popular phenomenon, but did you know that it is being used in agile project management as well? Having the best people in the team gives you the opportunity to sit back and relax while they complete their work on time with autonomy and all you need to do is make sure that things are done right before they deliver it. Agile management is in part a reliance on the team members who are experts in knowing their jobs and tasks. The role of a leader is important to help them and guide them through working together but they do not need an eye kept on them all the time to make sure they are on track. If you have the right people for the right jobs, there is no need to constantly monitor them but you have to build trust, with performance evaluation done by observation or more formally does play some role in getting the project completed on time.

These evaluations need to be done so that you know everyone is on track and no one is deviating from the goal of the project. The goal needs to be reviewed every day by the agile leader to the team so they do not forget it and work with complete motivation. Self-driven teams are not free of management but instead, the managers interact with the team members to receive the updates. They do not have to look at them to judge whether they are doing the work or not, but communication is the main key to help them reach the goal easily and without any delays. The emergence of interaction needs to begin before the project starts so a good connection can be made within the organization. When the internal environment of a company is good and friendly, then the team members do want to work with motivation and all the efficiency to show their best work.

Teamwork in Agile Project Management

When the team is working together to reach the same goal then it is highly likely that the project will be successful. If the team collaborates well and understands the need for the project and how it can help the organization, then there is little which can stop them from performing to the level which is required to reach the deadline. They all work together so that tasks are managed and even if someone is lacking in some of the skills, then they would use their own expertise to get on with their work as well. This is what agile project management requires for the team members to have amongst them while they are working on the project. A project cannot be completed by only person ever, which is why the concept of team building, where diverse people help each other to reach a common goal for the organization, comes into play.

A high level of performance can be achieved by such teams who make sure to finish the programming and the work by the end of the day through helping each other out. The backlog items are covered by anyone who finishes the daily tasks early, rather than sits idle so that there is no loss of time on the tasks which can all be done before their deadlines. They may even work on the next day's tasks to get ahead with the work.

Meeting together and communicating is an essential part of the agile teamwork system. It helps everyone to discover new ideas and encourages them to share these while working with each other. Even if someone is not used to speaking up, the system gives them the opportunities to do so and if anyone is facing a problem they can ask openly. The scrum leader encourages the team in talking with each other so that the messages and the goal can be clear.

Suppose there is someone who is not communicating and working on something that is not required due to a misconception, then it will be a waste of their energy and time as well as for the project, which can lead to delays because the right work is not being completed. When you talk amongst the team you will all be clear on what work is a priority along with adding new features to the product and staying on track with what you should be doing.

The team members can also talk with the product owner to better understand the features of the product and how these should work and what should be the response rate of the product, the criteria and so on. No one needs to play the part of an intermediary with agile project management so they have direct communication with every person, management or not.

Small Tasks

Where there are smaller tasks when you coordinate frequently and without any hassle, these can be allocated to those who have already completed their work beforehand. There are always people in the team who complete their work before anyone else but do not like to sit idle so they can help the ones which may be having problems in getting their work done. Among the team members, if you feel like someone is there who needs training, you need to identify their training needs to make sure they are addressed and help them learn to do better in the organization. It will not only enhance their own performance but give more confidence when they know all the work, which can help retain them in the organization and they will work with greater motivation.

Handing off the work to someone else is a short-term solution and to develop the team you need to train staff and share skills and expertise so that when it is time for testing, you can ensure everyone can contribute fully. The project manager also needs to have a good understanding of all aspects of the software too, as he will be accountable to the senior management and asked about the project.

When the team members work with each other, they get to know the problems of others quickly time and are usually willing to share their knowledge. They go out of the way to help each other due to the agile project management system which encourages them to collaborate rather than work on their own, knowing that they all need to report on the tasks at the end of the day. The team is ahead of the game when they are working with each other, providing a good environment for all to produce great work.

Manageable Mix of Teams

When there is a new sprint ahead, it is necessary that you see it in relation to the size of the whole project and then manage the team and schedule accordingly. Consider whether you need more people in the team and then there will be another look for a team member who can fit in. You have to find a programmer who can help and test the complete procedure to give the okay signal to the team that they are working well with each other. Each team member needs to be honest and open with each other in order to complement their skills, so you have to bring many of them together encouraging them to get along and work for the project and company as a whole. Avoid those people whom you think won't be able to cope with agile management, no matter how good their work might be if they could disrupt the team. You can teach the work to someone who does not know it but you cannot modify the basic behavior of someone who is not willing to fit in the team and does not like to work in a group. It can be challenging sometimes to get all of them together and on the same track. Sometimes they can have misunderstandings which can bring about a pause in the work and you have to bring them back together and on track, even if there is a short delay in the submission of daily tasks. All of them need to be ahead of schedule so that there is time left for the testing part and corrections if needed. You cannot meet the deadline at all when you are still developing the project because it leaves a negative impression for the company and the entire team that they could not coordinate well. All of the team members need to embrace working with each other and avoid mistakes.

Agile project management does not compromise on the rules and regulations of the company but makes sure that the flow of work is easy so that the quality of work generated is very high. According to research on this topic, if you give full autonomy to the team members and give them the deadline, they tend to work better at their own pace with those coworkers which they fit with the best. So, when a sense of teamwork is built they are given the authority to do the work in the area that they are an expert in.

Teamwork plays a huge role in agile project management because, without it, the project is incomplete. If you do not have a good team which does not know how to working together then there can be a chance that the project may fail to reach the deadline. Each member needs to understand each other, being friendly and cooperative so that the work can be interesting for them and benefit the company in the other ways too.

Adopting Agile Project Management

When looking at the projects, there will be the question of when and how to start the company working towards agile project management? Should they take on small projects or big ones to start applying agile techniques to? Agile project management is about spreading the system throughout the organization where everyone has some contribution in making the project successful for the company. A lot of companies start small because they are scared about the system working for them, but the system is not at the fault rather the people who are working with the system may not know how to operate it well. A system is never to be blamed but it is all about the people who operate it, knowing the risk of how important it can become when you are taking on a project which needs to be completed efficiently by the deadline.

Another question which may arise is whether to adopt it one project at a time or mid-project for those already in development. Some organizations may start working with an overlapping system where they would have multiple agile small projects so that they can be efficient and have experience over it, but that would not be wise. It is always better to start small whether it is a new business or a new system in your business. Do not confuse yourself with the various techniques, the advice would be to go into small patterns to understand the system slowly at first and then use it for bigger projects which you can handle more easily, without panicking. The main reason is that you cannot take risks with the big projects because if they fail, then it can portray a bad image for the company in the market. It is the image and reputation which the company sustains in the market which is in the mind of potential clients. If the stakeholders know that you do not deliver the work on time and that too is a fault, then who would want to get their products from you?

It is obvious that due to the competitive environment of the market, the company may not be doing so well using the traditional project management, which is why instead of consulting with any lawyer that you may be going bankrupt, it is better to try the agile project management system which can help you in adopting new ways of management and making the way for people to work simpler than before. The growth may be slow but there will be growth over a period of time as you learn all the techniques of agile project management which can be much more efficient.

When you start on small projects, it is less expensive for you to hire in some expertise as you can have the same transitions to agile management, but at a cheaper rate. You will not be able to gain so much out of it but the learning would not be extravagant. It will teach you a lot of new ways of handling the techniques and understanding the terms of a project with a scrum master and a trainer. The internal growth and adoption of new ways will be worked upon with this expertise to help you grow within the market and improve your profile. There will be some mistakes which you would make initially, but there is a learning curve for everyone and early mistakes lead to the success of the organization at some point. If you know what you are aiming for then you will reach a point where you would no longer need the help and would be able to sustain things yourself in the best manner.

When you start with small projects, you are likely to get early success, which can add confidence that you do know the techniques and you are ready to take on a big project. It can guarantee you that your company and the team members are ready to face the competitors on a larger scale, reaching for greater success in no time when you take on large projects. The small projects work as a backup for you in your portfolio when you bid on large projects. You can avoid big risks and have the authority over the projects, enabling yourself for more successful projects in future. The team can find out many easy ways to achieve their tasks, along with gaining the experience of learning new things from the projects.

Scrum Meetings and Procedures

When you are working on a project, it is vital to bring the team along with you which is why having regular scrum meetings is important. These were mentioned earlier in this book but here we will look at them in more detail. Scrum meetings are held every day for projects which are large in order to maintain the communication between the leader and the team members. A single message for everyone to work on the common goal, knowing where they need to keep their focus and what is required. Integration, focus, work system and overlapping are discussed in the meeting. The scrum leader is appointed who belongs to the team but acts also as a technical contributor to all of the team. It could be a programmer, administrator, tester, designer or so on. The team members report to the scrum leader by the end of the day and then the product owner is updated by the scrum leader. However, the product owner has no restrictions on reaching out to individual team members anytime he/she wishes to. If you are chosen as a scrum leader, you basically play a role as a representative for the team members to get their work done along with helping them out with the project. There are some processes which need to be followed consistently by the scrum leader at the meetings on a daily basis which should be effective for the team.

Frequency of Meetings

The frequency of the meetings should be maintained without missing days in between so that it becomes a routine that everyone has to be on time and attend for updates on information or knowledge of the project. So, if they miss it, they may not be informed on the tasks for the day. The meeting does not need to be more than 15 minutes long unless there are specific concerns of the team members which need to be addressed. The meetings should try to stick to the topic, have a consistent schedule and timing. Everyone needs to know that they will be expected to attend these meetings. The meetings are not there to solve all the problems so make sure you do not end up discussing the issues, but it is to remind everyone of the goal and target which everyone shares. Both pending and completed tasks need to be discussed in the meetings. If there are any issues within a team, individuals can see the scrum leader in their office to discuss these. A problem which one team may have would not necessarily be relevant to someone else so do not waste their time. It may be wiser to visit the scrum leader's office and sort it out then, so it does not affect anyone else's work.

Agenda

Every meeting in an organization has an agenda to follow but what is the agenda for these 15 minutes every day? Well, you still need to have a proper agenda for it so that it includes any of the information which can be useful and help the team members in working efficiently, answering questions which are not always asked but could be an issue while they are working.

Each team member needs to answer certain questions that:

- What did they do yesterday?
- What are your goals for today?
- What are the obstacles which you faced yesterday and how would you overcome them?

These three questions need to be addressed by every member, which they must answer and cannot say that they did not face anything during the entire day. The last question could work as a contribution for the scrum leader to know whether a person can solve their own problems or that he needs to be around some of the time to support them. Try not to name and shame while you are mentioning issues you observe, which may create a bigger problem in the future for the project. Another thing to try to do during the meeting is give equal importance to all the team members and do not just look at one person while you are delivering your message. You have to maintain eye contact with everyone while discussing the agenda so that everyone is on the same page. Any backlog issue which needs to be discussed so it can be worked on further should be mentioned, along with reminding the team about the deadline which is to be met. If they complete their tasks on a daily basis then they will be able to reach the target, so make sure that they report to you by the end of the day that they have completed that day's tasks to be sure that work is not late for the project.

It is through the scrum meetings that you can make sure that everyone is doing the work and you are getting a fair response from every individual. For very large projects or even some smaller ones, you cannot ignore a team member if you feel like a certain individual is not performing well. The iterations can help you in reviewing performance, looking at more formal evaluations and backlog issues. There will be fewer formal meetings under agile project management systems because when there is a more casual environment, it helps in getting on with the work better than any other management trick which you may apply. You can never force someone to work, which is why it is important that you ensure everyone is motivated and when there is leniency you have to take complete responsibility for this, without any complaints from a higher authority because it disturbs the entire project and the temperament of the team.

Agile Project Checklist

A checklist is always important for you to measure whether you have missed anything important while you are working on a project. A project cannot be done without planning and control, which is why you must make sure that you are marking off the tasks which you have completed and those which remain, so you can complete the project before the deadline. Deadlines are critical to meet for the project, to protect the reputation of your company, also ensuring you provide quality work as required by the stakeholders. Finishing the project on time assures the stakeholders that the work has been organized and they can check on the progress to make sure that quality has been provided by the team and is satisfied by the leads. The following checklist will help you make sure that you are on track with projects, not missing out a single thing so you do not have to compromise on the quality of the products or the work which you provide to the stakeholders.

✓ Following the 12 main principles

✓ Planning an agile project

✓ Tracking the project

✓ Knowing the events and sprints or iterations of the project

✓ Understating the scope of agile lifecycle

✓ Implementing the lifecycle

✓ Holding daily meetings

✓ Knowing the agenda of meetings

✓ Consistent approach to learning for all

✓ Transferring knowledge to other team members

- ✓ Working together
- ✓ Understanding the conceptual phase
- ✓ Following the inception
- ✓ Moving to production
- ✓ Keeping updated and monitoring
- ✓ Moving to transition
- ✓ Testing the system
- ✓ Making changes if required
- ✓ Production of the system and feedback
- ✓ Retirement of the system within conditions.

✓ Reviewing and improving the training of team members.

These key factors will help you to attain the best result when you will see all of them ticked off, you will be satisfied as a leader that you have managed to complete the project using agile project management techniques. Understanding agile project management is not hard but when it comes to implementation then there can be obstacles which may be difficult to manage. It will be more so for the manager who is new to the system but for someone who has handled a lot of projects, they won't find it hard to implement them on a daily basis.

Conclusion

A huge demand for agile project management rose in the marketplace a few years back when it emerged, with an urgency to adopt it as soon as possible for those organizations which used it as a test and were successful at achieving their projects more effectively than their competitors. As technology advances, there are changes which are meant to come into the processes and the entire organization has to go through these changes which some people may resist. The change and the processes being changed in the organization can make some people leave their job, but if they wish to accept the challenges, there is nothing which a person cannot learn. There are techniques and methods which are included in this book which will help you go through a project with agile management, even if you are trying it for the first time. All of the more successful companies in the market are currently following agile project management, depending upon their own genres which they excel in.

The systems that are updated and the services being provided to the clients are determined according to their own needs, which help retain them as customers for the longer term, organizations then do not need to depend on anyone but themselves for success, and it is in their own hands to meet the needs of the stakeholders. When they produce something which is wished for by the stakeholders, it is obvious that will like it and come back for similar work again, along with recommending the business to others which would contribute to the growth of the company.

If organizations do not adopt changes then it can be hard for them to survive, due to the customers' demands which change every day. An organization must modify itself to meet these as the market has become customer driven, where it is necessary that the client is satisfied with your service. Meeting a customer's needs is a critical factor for success in a competitive market. If you are not offering something which the client needs, then there will be some other similar company which will be doing so and the client will shift to them to get the services they want and need. Agile project management helps companies reach for success which working with on projects in the most effective ways, accepting change and helping the team work together to reach the end goal.

Everyone in the organization is aware of the goal, being clear on their tasks so that they are able to perform to the best of their abilities, showing that a project can be done better through collaboration and agile techniques. Help your company and yourself so you can achieve more with the help of agile project management and you can flourish in the future, creating more opportunities for success in the market.

Finally, if you enjoyed this book, please take the time to share your thoughts and post a review on Amazon. It would be greatly appreciated!

www.ingramcontent.com/pod-product-compliance
Lightning Source LLC
Chambersburg PA
CBHW070257230526
45470CB00002B/622